CONTENTS

THE SECRET BOOK COMPANY

©2019
The Secret Book Company
King's Lynn
Norfolk PE30 4LS

ISBN: 978-1-912171-72-9

Written by:
Gemma McMullen
Edited by:
Harriet Brundle
Designed by:
Matt Rumbelow
Ian McMullen

A catalogue record for this book
is available from the British Library

Words in **bold** can be found in the glossary on page 24.

THE SOLAR SYSTEM

The Solar System is the Sun and all of the objects that **orbit**, or go around it. Eight planets orbit the Sun, including our home, Earth.

THE SUN

en

THE
SOLAR
SYSTEM

THE SOLAR SYSTEM

It is not only planets that orbit the Sun.
Many moons, dwarf planets and **asteroids**
also make up our Solar System.

ASTEROIDS

PLANETS

WHAT IS THE SUN?

THE SUN

The Sun is a star. Stars are giant balls of gas that are very hot and bright. The Sun is a yellow star. The centre of the Sun is its hottest point.

Some parts of the Sun are not as hot as the rest. These parts are called Sun spots.

SUN SPOTS

CREATING LIFE

The Sun lights and heats all the planets, including planet Earth. All living things need the Sun.

Without the Sun, Earth would be dark and cold. Plants could not grow so animals would have no food.

EQUATOR

The middle of the Earth is called the **equator**. It is the closest part of the Earth to the Sun and is the hottest part of the planet.

WHERE DOES THE SUN GO AT NIGHTTIME?

TAKES ONE DAY

As well as going around the Sun, Earth is always spinning. It takes 24 hours (one day) for the Earth to turn around completely.

We cannot see the Sun at night because the Earth has spun around. The Sun is lighting the other side of the globe.

THE MOON

THE MOON

THE EARTH

The Moon orbits Earth, as well as the Sun. It is much smaller than the Sun but looks a similar size in the sky because it is much closer to Earth than the Sun is.

12

The Moon has no light of its own. It is bright in the sky because the Sun lights it.

SOLAR ECLIPSE

Sometimes the Moon moves in front of the Sun. This is called a solar eclipse. As the Sun's light and heat is being blocked, Earth becomes cold and dark for a short time.

THE MOON

THE EARTH

THE SUN

During a solar eclipse, animals get ready to go to sleep because they think that nighttime is coming.

POWERFUL SUN

The Sun is very powerful. Its strong rays can burn our skin. It is important to protect ourselves from the Sun with clothing and lotion.

Looking directly at the Sun could damage your eyes.

16

It is best to stay in the shade during the hottest part of a summer's day.

WHICH PLANETS ARE CLOSEST TO THE SUN?

There are eight planets in our Solar System. All of the planets orbit the Sun. Mercury is the closest planet to the Sun. Its surface is very hot.

Earth is the third closest planet to the Sun. The planets which are furthest away are called Uranus and Neptune.

MERCURY

EARTH

Uranus and Neptune are very cold planets.

THE OTHER STARS

There are many other stars that we can see in the sky. They look smaller than the Sun but that is because they are further away.

A GROUP OF STARS IS CALLED A GALAXY.

BLUE
SUPERGIANT

THE SUN

Stars can be different colours. The largest stars are blue or red. Smaller stars, like our Sun, are yellow.

21

SUPER SUN!

1 It takes about eight minutes for the Sun's light to reach Earth.

eight minutes

2 The Romans called the Sun 'sol'. In Ancient Greece the Sun was called 'Helios'.

3 Our Sun is part of a galaxy called the Milky Way.

4 In the past, people believed that the Sun orbited the Earth, rather than the other way around.

23

GLOSSARY

asteroids	large rocks which orbit the Sun
dwarf planets	very small planets
Equator	the imaginary line around the Earth that is an equal distance from the North and South Poles
globe	planet Earth
orbit	move around

INDEX

PHOTO CREDITS

Photocredits: Abbreviations: l-left, r-right, b-bottom, t-top, c-centre, m-middle. All images are courtesy of Shutterstock.com.
Front Cover — Markus Gann, 1 – Denis Rozhnovsky, 2/3 – Vadim Sadovski, 4bg – fluidworkshop, 5 inset – Denis_A, 6 – Denis Rozhnovsky, 7 – Twin Design, 8/9 – ParabolStudio, 9 Inset – Ismagilov, 10 bg – carlos castilla, 10 inset – gst, 11 – Angela Waye, 12 – muratart, 13 – Sergey Nivens, 14 bg – Igor Zh., 15r – mrotchua, 15 Inset – Sylvie Bouchard, 16 bg – Anna Omelchenko, 16 Inset – Gelpi JM, 17 – Monika Gniot, 18/19 – Christos Georghiou, 20 – Triff, 21 – Triff, 22 TR – Ruslan Grechka, 22 BL – Nejron Photo, 23 T – AstroStar, 23 BL – Georgios Kollidas, 24 BG – Vadim Sadovski, 24 Inset – Vadim Sadovski. All facts, statistics, web addresses and URLs in this book were verified as valid and accurate at time of writing. No responsibility for any changes to external websites or references can be accepted by either the author or publisher